Worms, Worms, Worms

Carter Hayn

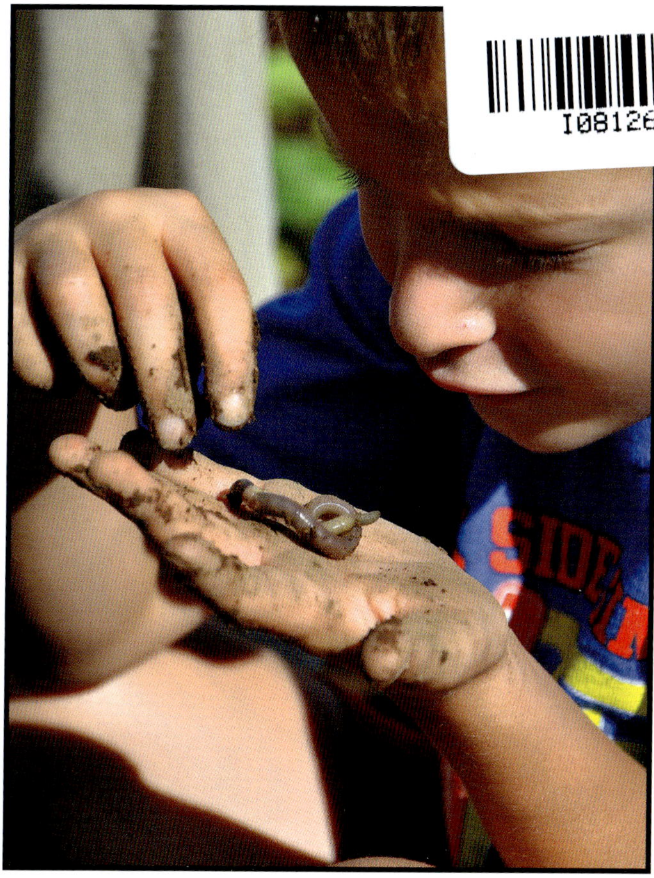

Rosen REAL READERS

Rosen Classroom™
New York

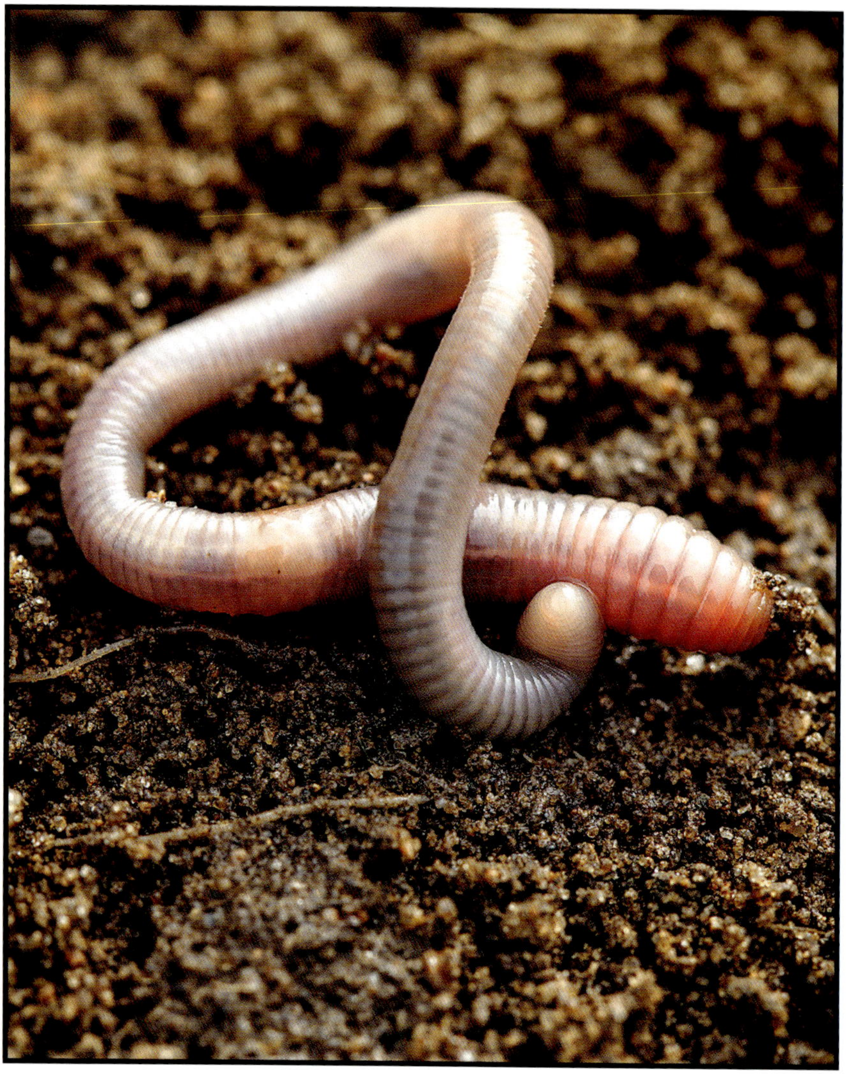

This is a worm.

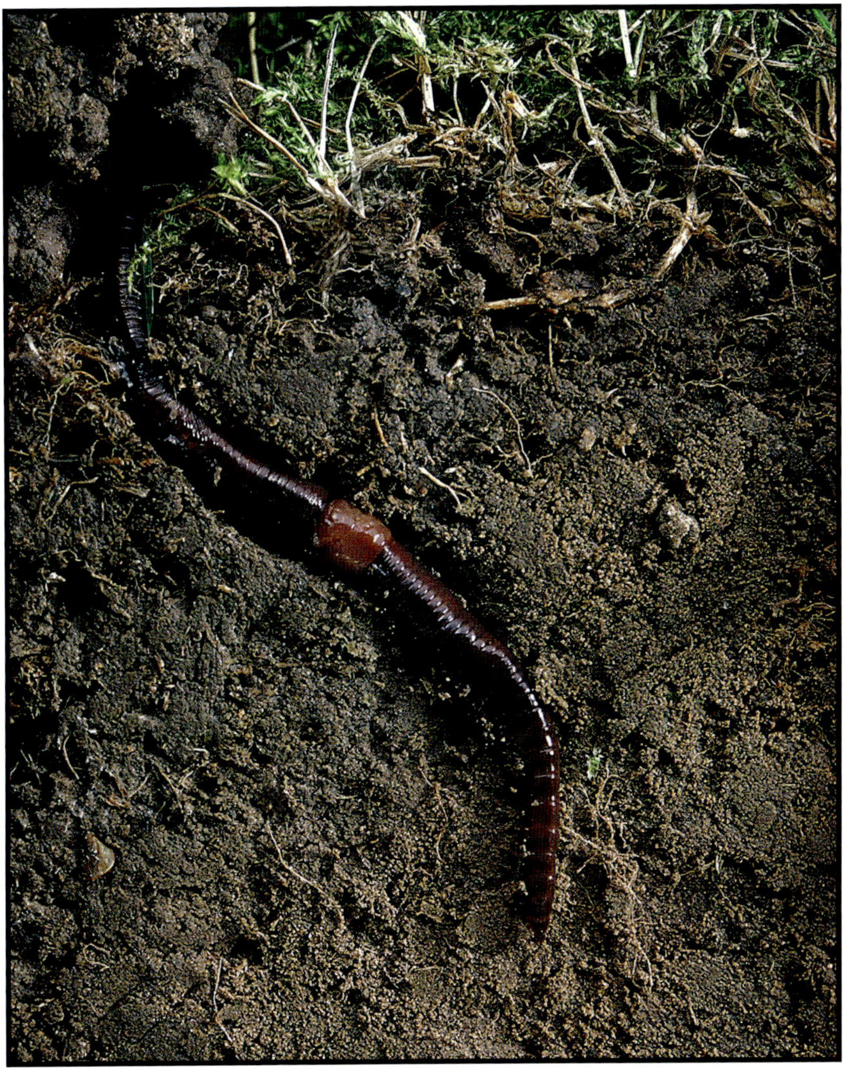

Worms live in the ground.

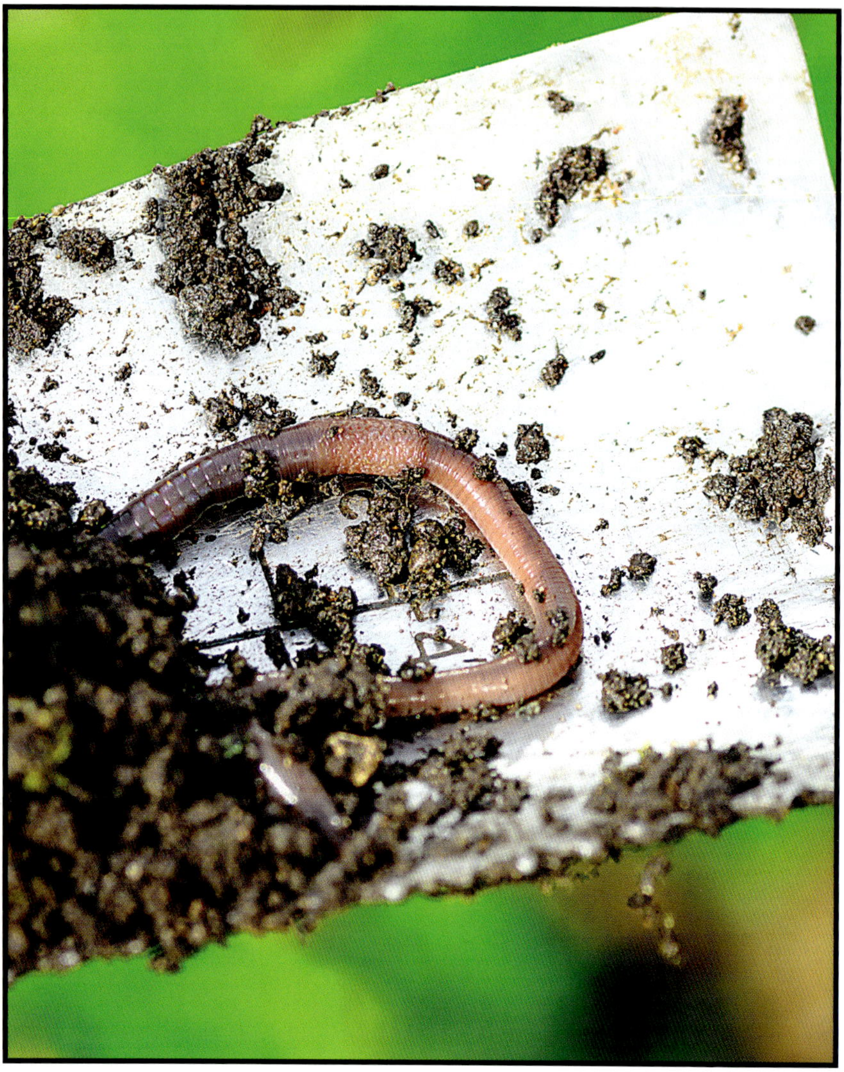

Worms are good for the soil.

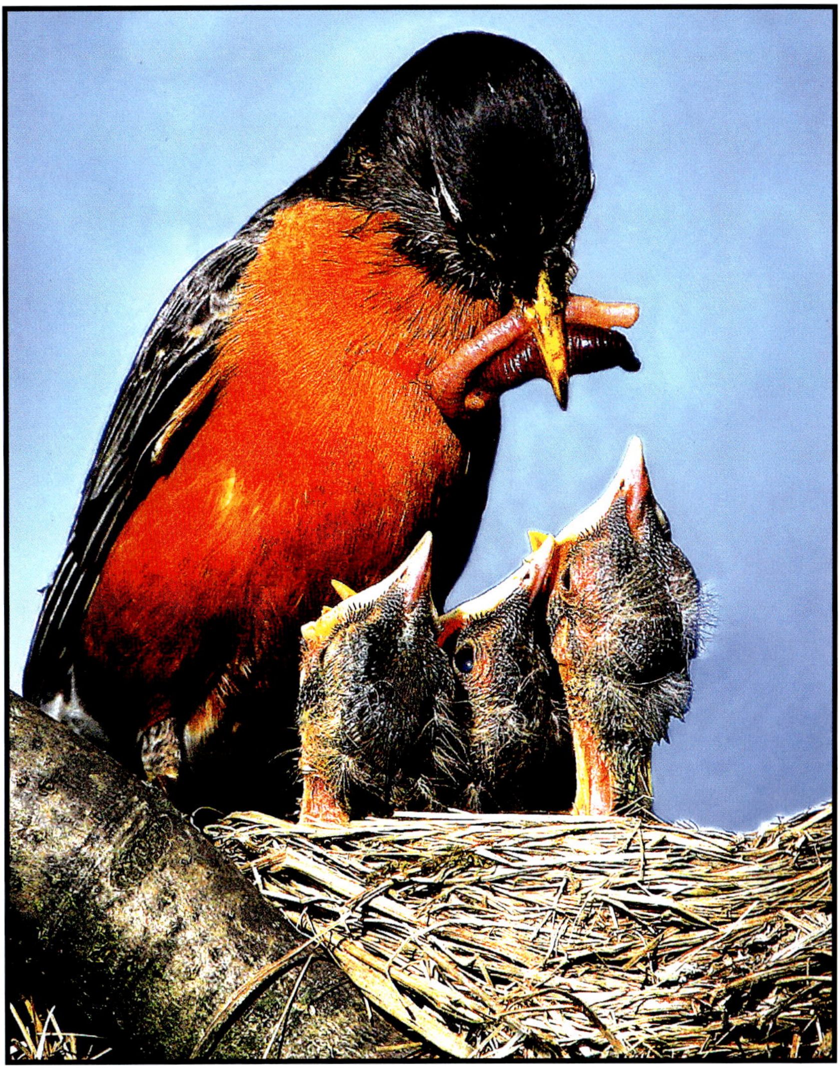

Birds eat worms.

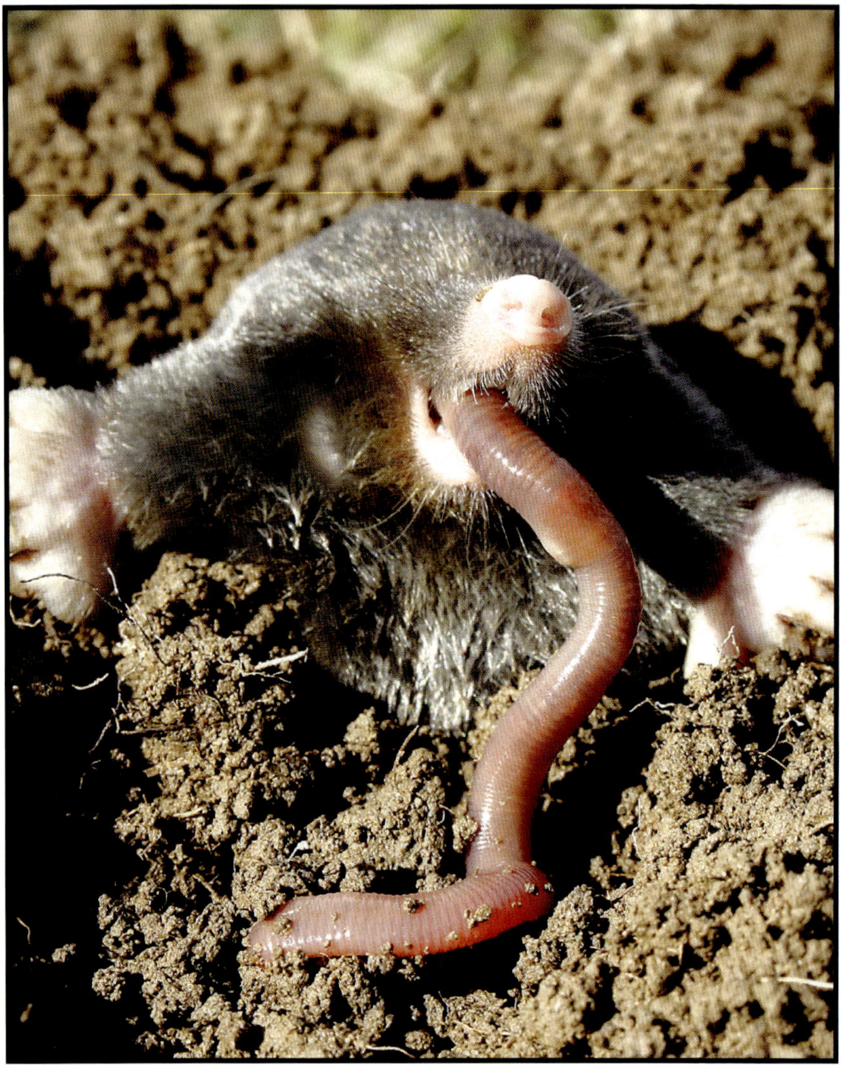

Moles eat worms, too.

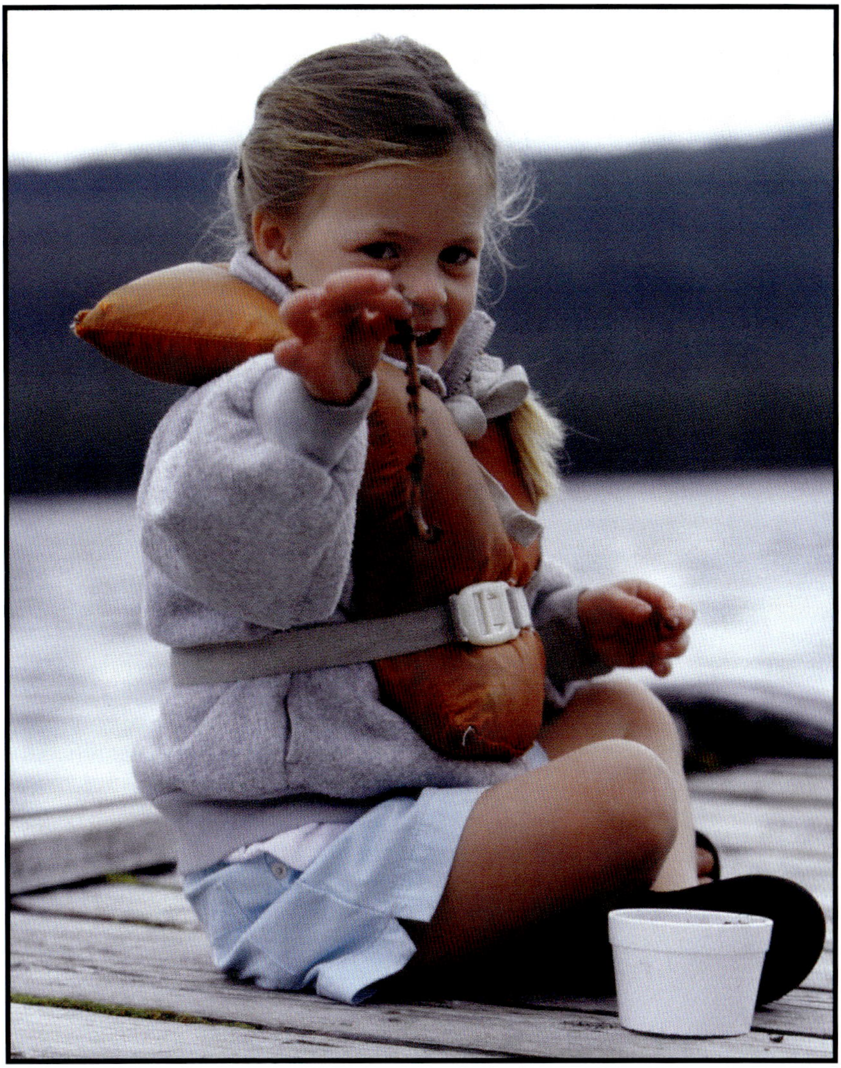

I use worms to fish.

Words To Know

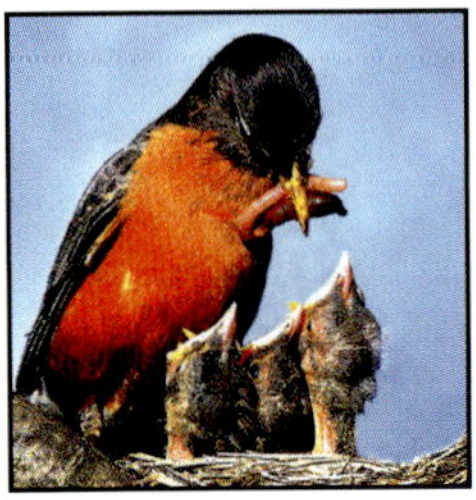

bird

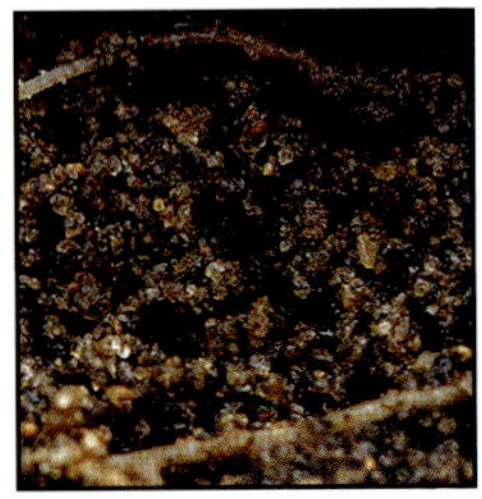

ground

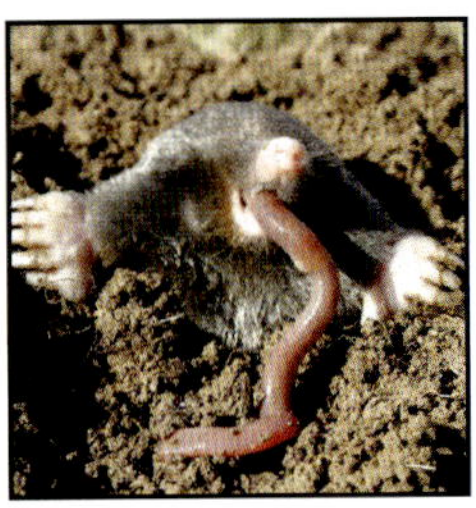

mole

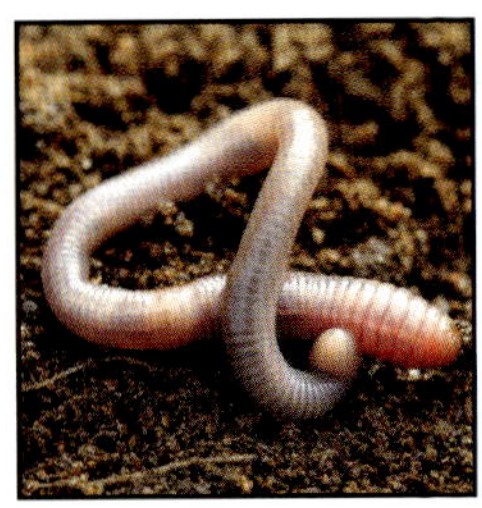

worm